Original title:
Seedlings of Thought

Copyright © 2025 Creative Arts Management OÜ
All rights reserved.

Author: Ethan Prescott
ISBN HARDBACK: 978-1-80566-674-5
ISBN PAPERBACK: 978-1-80566-959-3

Roots of Reflection

In a garden of my mind, we dig,
Finding thoughts that dance and jig.
A worm with glasses, taking notes,
Laughs at ideas that take boat trips.

Planting dreams in rows so neat,
We plan a feast of silly treats.
With soil that's rich in giggles and glee,
We nurture nonsense, wild and free.

Sprouts of Curiosity

What happens when a seed takes flight?
It starts to wonder, day and night.
A sprout with questions fills the air,
Asking, 'Are we beans or just a dare?'

The sunbeam grins, the raindrop sings,
Sprouts explore the oddest things.
Chasing shadows, they trip and fall,
Laughing loud, they summon all.

The Nurturing of Insights

In pots of wonder, wisdom grows,
With quirky thoughts like dancing toes.
A wise old tree once told a joke,
But I still can't recall, just smoke!

Watering ideas with silly songs,
Mixing helpings of right and wrongs.
Our garden's filled with laughter's might,
Where every blunder feels just right.

Tiny Buds of Wisdom

Little buds with questions bright,
Pondering life in sheer delight.
'Why did the chicken cross the lane?'
To tickle thoughts, or was it pain?

They giggle at the dandelion's show,
And wonder why the sky is low.
Growing wise, they trade their puns,
For giggly moments, there are tons.

Budding Journeys

Tiny ideas sprout and dance,
In a pot of dreams, they prance.
Some are silly, some take flight,
Creating giggles, pure delight.

In a garden fresh and bright,
Thoughts are germinating right.
One says, "What if cats could talk?"
Another yells, "Let's build a rock!"

They tumble and roll in the sun,
Mixing stories, oh what fun!
Each twist and turn, a new surprise,
Where laughter echoes, wisdom lies.

Shimmering Insights

Twinkling thoughts like stars above,
Wobble wiggly, like a dove.
One idea whispers with a grin,
"Shall we bake a cake with tin?"

Bubbling giggles, thoughts collide,
Each a treasure, spread wide.
What if toasters needed shoes?
And socks were made of bright hues?

A jumble of colors, a mix of cheer,
Sprinkling laughter, far and near.
With every chuckle, new hope grows,
Like daisies popping up through snows.

Melting Pot of Ideas

In a pot, ideas melt and sway,
Comedic flavors come out to play.
One imagines frogs in bow ties,
Doing the waltz, oh what a surprise!

Thoughts stew together, simmering bright,
Mushrooms of laughter take off in flight.
Maybe penguins wear fancy hats,
Or bicycles played by jumping spats!

Stirring and swirling with each new jest,
Creativity gives every guess a fest.
From giggles to belly laughs, we melt,
In a soup of joy, a warmth felt.

Breaths of New Beginnings

A wind of whimsy, fresh and light,
Blows through ideas, taking flight.
One says, "What if fish could dance?"
Another giggles at a chicken's prance.

With every breath, a chuckle grows,
New beginnings in joyful throes.
What about trees in rollerblades?
Or flamingos throwing parades?

Each inhale brings a zany thought,
Unlocking the laughter that can't be bought.
In this world of playful schemes,
Humor springs forth like wild dreams.

Hues of Hope

A tiny sprout, a green delight,
Dancing in the morning light.
It dreams of trees, so tall and grand,
But first must conquer this small land.

With sunlight's kiss and rain's embrace,
It wiggles up, quickening its pace.
A little leaf with lots to say,
In whispers soft, it finds its way.

A garden gnome just shakes his head,
'You think you're grand? You're just well-fed!'
But little sprout, with childlike glee,
Retorts, 'I'm more than what you see!'

So here in dirt, the laughter grows,
With every breeze, a tale it sows.
Though small, it's mighty in its quest,
To be the best, just like the rest!

Boughs of Brilliance

Oh, look at me, I'm quite the tree!
With branches wide, a sight to see.
But wait! I'm only just a sprout,
Pretending grand, yet full of doubt.

With laughter in the summer air,
I sway and shimmy without a care.
My leaves are green, my trunk is thin,
But in my heart, the wind's my kin.

The squirrels tease, they run about,
'Is that your height? Come on, sprout out!'
Yet I just giggle, what a show,
A little wood in the breeze, I grow!

When autumn comes, I'll make a stance,
With colors bright, I'll lead the dance.
But for now, I'm just having fun,
So green and goofy, soaking sun!

Moments of Stillness

In the garden, time stands still,
A thought bobbles like a cork on a hill.
The flowers whisper their sweet secrets,
While shadows spin in charming duets.

The ants debate on who's the best,
While ladybugs go on a quest.
But in this peace, I soak it in,
Staring at clusters, letting thoughts spin.

A butterfly flits, it stops to peek,
Says, 'Little guy, you're quite unique!'
But I just nod, with soil on my nose,
In moments still, I've found my pose.

So here I bask 'neath the sun and dirt,
In laughter, giggles—oh what a flurt!
Though time may move with swift and haste,
In quiet joy, I find my taste!

Initial Sparks

One little thought, oh what a start,
It tickles the mind, a tiny dart.
Like a match that caught a breeze,
It dances 'round with playful ease.

The doodles start, a scribble here,
A spark of ideas, nothing to fear.
But as it grows, it starts to swing,
And then it takes off—what a fling!

A burst of laughter, a moment bright,
Ideas soar, like kites in flight.
But wait a sec; just where'd they go?
In zany form, they put on a show!

So chase the flickers, let them play,
With giggles, shimmer, and bright ballet.
Each initial spark, a joy to find,
Lights up the corners of the mind!

Growth of Contemplation

In the garden of my mind, they sprout,
Ideas wiggle, dance about.
Worms of wisdom wriggle free,
Tickling thoughts, oh what a spree!

Glimmers, glances, light and fun,
Every pondering thought has begun.
With laughter, they bounce and skip,
On sunshine's rays, they take a dip.

Chasing clouds with giggle fits,
As each new notion gently sits.
Building castles in the air,
Till they crumble, without a care!

So in my head, they twist and twirl,
A merry dance, a playful whirl.
With every glance and silly jest,
Contemplations turn to laughter's quest.

Dandelions of Introspection

Puffs of fluff with thoughts to share,
Blowing wishes into the air.
Each little seed, a hope to chase,
In the wind, they find their place.

Round and round, they spin and fly,
Wishing on each passerby.
With giggles, they dance in the breeze,
Tickling minds like teasing bees.

Silly thoughts that make us grin,
From the chaos, we'll begin.
Each little whisper floating high,
Is a chuckle on the sly.

So here's to thoughts that puff and play,
Sprouting joy in their own way.
With snickers, snorts, and laughter loud,
We'll share them with the gathering crowd.

Gale of Imagination

An idea caught in a sudden wind,
Swirled in giggles, it spins and grins.
A whirlwind of laughs, a cyclone of cheer,
From the depths of thought, they appear.

Floating high, like kites on strings,
Oh, the joy that inventiveness brings!
With silly shapes and quirky sights,
A festival of colorful delights.

Every twist, a burst of surprise,
Who knew thoughts could materialize?
In the funny game of mind's play,
Imagination has found its way!

So grab hold tight as the gale blows through,
Riding the waves of the new and the true.
Through tornadoes of chuckles, we spin and flirt,
In laughter's embrace, our minds are made to skirt.

Delicate Flights of Fancy

On wings of whimsy, thoughts take flight,
Delicate fancies, oh what a sight!
Each fluttering notion, light as a feather,
We chase our dreams together, forever.

With imagination's playful grace,
We sail through clouds at a dizzying pace.
Laughter bubbles like a fizzy drink,
In this fanciful world, we blink.

From dainty wishes to outlandish schemes,
Crafting a tapestry sewn with dreams.
They're quirky, cheap, a real delight,
These playful flights, oh what a night!

So let us spread our mirthful wings,
Dance with joy, as laughter sings.
In the world of thoughts, we prance and glide,
In delicate flights, let joy be our guide.

Cultivating Clarity

In a garden where ideas grow,
I plant my thoughts in tidy rows.
With watering cans full of dreams,
I chuckle at how silly it seems.

Weeds of doubt sprout like bad puns,
Pull them up—oh, this is fun!
Sunshine smiles on my quirky schemes,
Laughter blooms in a field of memes.

Each thought a flower, bold and bright,
Colorful chaos, simply a sight.
Even the worms join in the cheer,
Wiggling around, they're always near.

So dig and delve in the playful mess,
Unruly thoughts, I'll gladly bless.
In my mind's garden, there's no defeat,
Just whimsical wonders and thoughts that compete.

Roots of Creativity

Roots intertwine beneath the ground,
Where giggles and guffaws can be found.
Branches sway with a comical twist,
Not a serious bud ever gets missed.

Each idea's a fruit, sweet and ripe,
Squirrels steal visions with endless hype.
I chase them around with a net made of dreams,
Hoping to catch their playful schemes.

Laughter bubbles up like sap in spring,
Every chuckle's a new little thing.
As shadows dance in the setting sun,
Roots hold secrets of joy and fun.

So let's plant thoughts like spaghetti in sauce,
Twirl them around; they're a playful gloss.
In this garden of whacky delight,
Creativity blooms, simply a sight!

Melodies of the Mind

Notes flutter lightly, like leaves in the breeze,
Each one a giggle, a melody with ease.
In my head, a chorus sings bright and clear,
Dancing around, it twirls with cheer.

Composers of chaos, we join and collide,
Ideas march out like a funny parade.
With rhythm and rhyme, the laughter flows,
As brainwaves twinkle, anything goes.

A joke's a tune, a thought's a song,
In this nutty orchestra, I can't go wrong.
Harmonize with whimsy, sway with the flow,
Sing out loud—let the world know!

With every outburst, the music grows bold,
A cacophony of giggles, joyous and gold.
So tap your toes, let your mind unwind,
For in this concert, humor you'll find!

Ebb and Flow of Inspiration

Like waves on the beach, ideas roll in,
Some are silly, some make me grin.
I ride the tide with a goofy face,
Sandy feet dancing in rhythmic grace.

The swell of whimsy pulls me along,
I surf on laughter, it feels like a song.
Caught in the currents of creative spree,
Who knew inspiration could tickle like tea?

Set the sails of your mind to explore,
Open horizons of laughter, not war.
With each rising wave, let the joy sprout,
Inspiration's playful is what it's about.

So paddle hard through the ups and the downs,
Wear a smile; let go of the frowns.
In this ebb and flow, find your delight,
For thoughts are like surfboards, ready for flight!

Hushed Revelations

In the garden where ideas play,
Whispers giggle, come what may.
Bouncing thoughts like rubber balls,
Tickling minds within four walls.

A cactus wears a jovial hat,
Sipping tea with a friendly rat.
Each secret blooms beneath the sun,
Who knew such fun could come undone?

The daisies dance in silly lines,
Debating if they're grapes or pines.
As petals laugh and twirl about,
The quiet sprouts all scream and shout.

When minds take flight like feathery kites,
In the crazy winds of wacky sights.
Smiles emerge on every vine,
In this jolly garden, life feels divine!

Petals of Perception

In a patch of blooms with zany flair,
Thoughts prance around, without a care.
Tulips tell stories in a hushed tone,
While marigolds giggle, fully grown.

A bee with glasses brings the news,
Buzzing about some hilarious views.
He claims to know the weather's fate,
But gets it wrong—oh, what a state!

The daisies set a dance-off scene,
Who can boast the funniest green?
They argue and tumble in the breeze,
Creating a spectacle that aims to please.

Each petal's a punchline in disguise,
Tickling the air, where whimsy lies.
With laughter painting every shade,
In the garden of humor, plans are laid!

Fertile Grounds of Thought

In the soil where laughter grows,
Curious minds strike funny poses.
Worms with jokes wriggle and squirm,
In this realm, silliness is the norm!

A sunflower trips over its stem,
Blushing at such an awkward gem.
While bluebells chuckle in delight,
Their giggles echo through the night.

The chives play hide and seek with the breeze,
Trying to catch their ticklish knees.
With roots that twist and turn around,
The wittiest blooms play tag on the ground!

So dig your head into this fun,
Where every thought's a silly pun.
In fertile grounds of joy unbound,
Laughter's harvest can be found!

Radiant Sparks of Insight

In a sparkly realm of bright ideas,
Thoughts shimmer like dancing sea otters.
With giggles aplenty and blinks of surprise,
Each bright notion wears a disguise.

Butterflies flutter with wisdom to share,
Tickling the brain with their playful flair.
A lightning bug hosts a comedy night,
Drawing echoes of laughter in moonlight.

The cacti wear shades, oh what a sight,
Cracking jokes under starlit light.
When insight strikes like a clumsy bee,
It buzzes away, just wait and see.

In the brilliance of each silly chat,
Ideas twirl in a feathery hat.
With radiant sparks igniting the air,
The fun never ends, let down your hair!

Pondering Frontiers

In the garden of my mind, I roam,
Chasing whispers of ideas I've yet to own.
I trip on thoughts that giggle and sneak,
Like butterflies wearing a tuxedo and peak.

The sun shines bright on my tangled schemes,
While rabbits debate the weight of dreams.
I ask a cactus if it knows a tune,
It rolls its eyes, says, "Only at noon!"

I planted a joke near the petunia bed,
Watered it with laughter; now it's well-fed.
A snail steals a glance, asks, "What's the fuss?"
I tell him, "Life's a race, but we're on a bus!"

Amidst these blooms of quirky cheer,
I gather my thoughts, they're like souvenirs.
Each idea a spark, each laugh a thread,
In this wild garden where nonsense is fed.

Tapestry of Thought

In the loom of my brain, threads intertwine,
A tapestry woven with ideas benign.
One says, "I'm a fish! I swim through the air!"
The other replies, "That's a bit rare!"

Colors collide like ducks in a pond,
Silly notions with a hint of the blonde.
I pluck a bright thought, it tickles my mind,
It laughs and it hops, leaving logic behind.

As I needle and thread through the fabric of wit,
A sock puppet chimes in, saying, "Don't quit!"
With each goofy stitch, I weave my delight,
Creating absurdity, oh what a sight!

When the sun sets down on my patchwork tales,
Each whimsical thought blooms, it never fails.
In the tapestry bright, humor takes flight,
A landscape of giggles, a feast for insight.

Unfurled Mysteries

In the shadows of questions, I roam about,
Chasing strange answers that don't leave a doubt.
I found a Noodle who wanted to rhyme,
It danced on my thoughts, sayin', "I'm quite sublime!"

With a wink and a quirk, my ideas take wing,
Singing like canaries, each one a fling.
A riddle once said, "Let's tickle the stars!"
They giggled and twinkled, wearing cute jars.

Under the sky where peculiar things hum,
I sought out the wise, and they all went 'Dumb!'
A clock once declared, "Time's up for the loud,"
I replied, "More laughter, let's make it proud!"

In circles of wonder, I play with the bizarre,
Like playful kittens who dream of a car.
Unfurled mysteries dance on my tongue,
Woven with humor, forever young.

Mosaic of Dreams

In the playful collage of my jumbled mind,
Are quirky creations of all kinds.
I found a bubble with wishes inside,
It giggled, said, "Let's go for a ride!"

Each piece of laughter forms a new hue,
Like jellybeans splattered in morning dew.
One dream's a sandwich, piled up high,
Flavored with nonsense, oh me, oh my!

Around me, the pixels of silly unfold,
A cat wearing boots, so brazen and bold.
I stuck on a thought, it wobbled and spun,
Said, "Life's just better if we dance and run!"

In this mosaic, bright, of whimsy and cheer,
Every thought a brushstroke, loud and clear.
With dreams as my palette, I paint with delight,
Creating a canvas of laughter so bright.

Renewing the Soil of Insight

In the garden of my mind,
Where odd ideas often twine,
I planted jokes, a quirky blend,
To see just what the smiles send.

With puns that dance like bumblebees,
And tickles carried by the breeze,
Each laughter's sprout, a treasure found,
Giggles sprouting all around.

A thought like rain on thirsty ground,
Grows silliness, profound, renowned,
The more I water with a grin,
The more the joy just spills within.

In this patch of playful dreams,
Where logic cracks and laughter screams,
I sow the seeds of silly schemes,
And harvest fun from crazy themes.

Roots of Resilience

In the soil of a playful fate,
I dig for laughs, they grow so great,
Each chuckle burrows down so deep,
And plants the joy I love to keep.

With roots that laugh when life gets rough,
They sprout resilience, nice and tough,
A wiggle here, a giggle there,
I find the strength when none seems fair.

Through storms of doubt and weed's charade,
I dance and twirl, I'm not afraid,
For when I fall, I spring back high,
With silly grace, I touch the sky.

So let my humor take its flight,
As roots entwine with pure delight,
A garden bright with whims unfurled,
Flourishing fun in a funny world.

Nurtured Dreams

In the garden where ideas play,
Silly visions dance all day,
I water them with giggles bright,
And watch them bloom in sheer delight.

Each dream a flower, bold and weird,
They whisper secrets, unfeared,
Some make me laugh, some make me ponder,
A funny world, a dreamland wonder.

I prune the weeds of doubt away,
And let laughter lead the way,
With every chuckle, blooms arise,
A wild patch under sunny skies.

So here I stand, a joyful host,
To dreams that tickle, tease, and boast,
In a quirky garden, strange yet grand,
Where nonsense grows at my command.

Whispered Musings

Among the thoughts that tiptoe high,
Whispers of humor pass me by,
With jokes that wiggle like a worm,
They rise up tall, so funny, firm.

In corners dim where shadows play,
Musings jiggle, shout hooray,
Each giggle buds like springtime cheer,
With ticklish vibes that draw me near.

As thoughts collide and laughter flows,
I gather smiles where humor grows,
A playful mind is far from bland,
With quirky dreams, this I have planned.

So let the whispers softly tease,
And spread the joy like dandelions in breeze,
In this garden of crazy schemes,
I nurture life with funny dreams.

The Voyage of New Ideas

A ship of wonders sails so high,
Its sails are bright, they catch the sky.
With thoughts like fish, they jump and play,
Turning boredom into a buffet.

The captain grins, a wacky chap,
In cargo holds, there's room for a nap.
Ideas catch the breeze so fine,
Upon this ship, all thoughts are mine.

The crew's a bunch of silly mates,
They juggle dreams and plate the fates.
With every wave, a laugh they find,
On this wild ride, oh so unconfined!

So off we go, it's plain to see,
Adventure's calling, join with me!
Let's sail away, with joy unfurled,
A wacky journey 'round the world!

Light and Shadow in the Mind

In a realm where shadows dance,
Ideas twirl in a silly prance.
A light bulb flickers, oh what a sight,
It winks and giggles, pure delight!

The thoughts are playful, bright and bold,
They leap and twirl, they never scold.
With a twist and a turn, they tease the brain,
Even the frowns begin to wane!

A shadow sneaks, it trips on a shoe,
While brilliant thoughts paint the sky so blue.
In this madcap game of light and dark,
Even the gloom can leave a mark!

So let's embrace this crazy show,
Where laughter blooms and ideas flow.
A jolly mix of shade and beam,
In the mind's playground, let's all dream!

Weaving the Fabric of Understanding

A loom of laughter, threads so bright,
I tug and pull, with all my might.
Each stitch a giggle, each knot a laugh,
Tangled ideas make the best path.

With colors vibrant, the pattern grows,
A tapestry of thoughts, goodness flows.
I stitch and snip, oh what a game,
Understanding wears a silly name!

The weaver grins, a cheeky sort,
He knots the nonsense, what a sport!
In fabric fine, the questions glide,
Twirling and whirling, side by side.

So gather 'round, let's weave away,
Crafting clarity in a wacky way.
With every loop, the jokes expand,
In this crazy quilt, we take a stand!

The Canvas of Contemplation

Imagine a canvas, blank and wide,
With splashes of color, wild in stride.
I dip my brush in a pot of cheer,
With each stroke, the giggles appear!

A splash of yellow, a streak of green,
Ideas pop like popcorn, keen.
Forget the lines, let chaos reign,
In this wild mix, there's no mundane!

The artist sways, a jester at heart,
Painting thoughts that jump and dart.
With every whim, I twist and spin,
Shaping laughter, deep within.

So grab your hues, let's paint the town,
In this world where smiles drown.
The canvas waits, let's make it sing,
With every thought, let the joy take wing!

Sprouts of Inspiration

In a garden of dreams, so bright,
Laughter sprouts with all its might.
A daisy tells a funny joke,
While the tomato plant starts to poke.

The carrots dance, don't take a chance,
While beans may twirl, it's quite a prance.
The radishes giggle, rolling round,
In this plot where joy is found.

They gather in the noon sun's glow,
Telling tales we all should know.
Chickens chuckle, hiding seeds,
The humor is all that one really needs.

Fragments of Imagination

In patches where the wild things grow,
A strawberry thinks it's a show.
The cabbage wears a funny hat,
Claiming it's not just any old sprat.

Pumpkins chat about their dreams,
Of who will win the veggie screams.
A squash starts telling tales of yore,
While the zucchini begs for more.

Silly sprites dance among the stems,
Creating laughter in the ends.
In this place where ideas bloom,
Even the weeds chase away the gloom.

Budding Perspectives

Oh, the parsley has quite the flair,
With comments that hang in the air.
Tomatoes gossip about the sun,
Declaring yesterday was just plain fun.

Cucumbers whisper secrets green,
In the funniest garden ever seen.
As kale rolls out a comic strip,
In this plot, there's no dull trip.

Radical radishes relish jokes,
While the peppers plan mischievous pokes.
Each sprout has a quirky tale,
As laughter dances down the trail.

Soil of Reflection

In the dirt where giggles decay,
Worms are plotting their next play.
Moles are busy, what a scene,
In the soil, they paint it green.

Ladybugs form a comedy troupe,
With ants joining in for a loop.
Reflections sprout from every nook,
As everything's funny in this book.

Dandelions spill their glee,
As wishes fly, just wait and see.
In this patch of mirthful ground,
Unexpected laughter can be found.

Echoes of the Mind

In the garden of my brain,
Ideas sprout, sometimes insane.
A rubber chicken calls my name,
Thoughts that tickle, never tame.

Silly visions fly like kites,
Doing loop-de-loops in flights.
A cactus sings a jaunty tune,
First in May, then in June.

With bouncy balls and funny hats,
My brain's a circus full of spats.
Clowns are juggling facts and jest,
I'm left to wonder, what's the best?

When ponderings grow wild and free,
I trip on laughter, can't you see?
Each giggle takes me for a ride,
In this funhouse of my mind, I glide.

Cultivating Visions

Planting seeds of wacky dreams,
Watering thoughts with silly streams.
A patch of joy, a bed of quirks,
Tending jokes and laughing smirks.

A garden gnome with roller skates,
Flips and spins while I just wait.
He whispers secrets that tickle me,
Of all the jokes 'neath the old tree.

We plant the puns, and they take root,
With every laugh, they bear sweet loot.
I prune the fears, let giggles grow,
In this farm of fun, what a show!

With trowels bright, we hoe the earth,
Uncovering treasures, a bumping berth.
A landscape lush with smiles and cheer,
Cultivating joy, always near.

Heartbeats of Awareness

I feel a pulse of funny sights,
A heartbeat echoes, pure delights.
Silly thoughts can make me grin,
Each giggle sneaks {right} on in.

Awareness twirls, a dizzy dance,
Thoughts in tutus take their chance.
With every chuckle, a new beat,
A symphony of humor, sweet.

I notice quirks that tease my mind,
A hopping bunny, one of a kind.
His antics cause my laughter swell,
In this rhythm, all is well.

So let my heartbeats guide me through,
A funny journey, fresh and new.
Awareness blooms in laughter's light,
In every tickle, joy takes flight.

Sprouting Curiosity

Oh, curious minds take daring leaps,
From questions deep to giggly heaps.
Why does the chicken cross the street?
To find a place where jokes retreat.

With each inquiry, my thoughts unfurl,
Exploring wonders, like a whirl.
A pickle in a sailor's hat,
My thoughts are swimming, just like that!

I wander through this maze of quirks,
Collecting giggles, dodging jerks.
Why do they laugh? I want to know,
Let's sprout adventures, let's go, go, go!

So here's to questions, big and small,
With every poke, I hear their call.
Curiosity, a cheeky sprout,
In this garden of fun, there's no doubt.

Whispers of the Quiet Mind

In the corners of my head, they play,
Ideas waltzing, oh so gay.
They trip and tumble, dance around,
Like squirrels searching for lost ground.

One thought wears a funny hat,
While another mocks a curious cat.
They giggle softly, making plans,
And argue over who steals fans.

The puns take root, a joke's been sown,
In this garden where quirks have grown.
Each chuckle bursts like popcorn's pop,
And all my brain can do is stop.

So here I sit, with laughter's plea,
As thoughts limp about, so carefree.
They jump and hop, a merry band,
Gathering mischief, oh so grand.

The Blossoming Ideas

Tulips sprout in my noodle land,
Funnier than any band!
They gossip 'bout a ticklish tree,
And stage a play for you and me.

A daffodil with socks so bright,
Dances while the others write.
They scribble jokes on upturned leaves,
Tickling minds like playful thieves.

Each jest emerges, bright and bold,
Wrapped in stories, ripe and gold.
Like flowers peeking from the dirt,
Waiting for laughter's happy flirt.

"Knock, knock," shouts the zinnia sprout,
And all the daisies join the shout.
They blossom forth with silly glee,
As every thought becomes a spree.

Germination of Dreams

In the soil of silly schemes,
Wiggle wiggle, giggle dreams.
They sprout like popcorn, bouncing high,
While butterflies dance in the sky.

A dream once told of pizza pies,
With toppings made of moonlit sighs.
They churn and twist, a cartoon fight,
Dancing under twinkling light.

From tiny seeds, absurdity grows,
With giggles tracing funny flows.
Each whimsical thought, a jumping bean,
A treasure trove of laughter's sheen.

Let's plant more, the giggle patch,
With dreams that twist and delightfully hatch.
From goofy roots, we're bound to sprout,
A garden where all jokes come out.

Echoes in the Garden

In this garden where laughter plays,
Echoes linger, in funny ways.
A cucumber jokes with a blushing rose,
While spinach giggles, turning toes.

Silly whispers bounce about,
Tickling every curious sprout.
The carrots chuckle, 'Take a bow!'
As broccoli shows off, 'Look at me now!'

The daisies dance, their petals sway,
Ticklish thoughts in bright disarray.
Each one's a burst of laughter's cheer,
Spilling joy that's always near.

An echo hums a cheeky tune,
With butterflies dancing under the moon.
In this garden where fun resides,
Giggles grow, and wisdom hides.

Yonder Horizons

In gardens wide, where giggles grow,
Tiny whispers chase the crow.
Curious sprouts with hats so tall,
Wondering how they might just fall.

A vision blooms with every rain,
Dancing thoughts like wild champagne.
Chasing bugs with slippery glee,
They plot a world that's bug-free!

Sunshine tickles their leafy friends,
Creating laughter that never ends.
They scheme beneath the great big sky,
With dreams of wings and how to fly.

And though it seems they're just so small,
These cheeky thoughts will stand up tall.
For even roots can break the mold,
In the tales of green and gold.

Ephemeral Epiphanies

In moments fleeting, ideas sprout,
Like daisies dancing all about.
A thought once shared, it jumps and jives,
A comedy that truly thrives.

Ticklish notions, wiggle and squirm,
As they play tag with a curious worm.
What's a detail here or there?
Just laughter tangled in the air!

A wink, a nod, a dash of zest,
Ideas wearing their Sunday best.
A glance, a grin, oh what a show,
As musings prance in manic tow.

These whims flit past in giggly streams,
With hopes that float in vibrant dreams.
In a world where chuckles reign,
Epiphanies dance like drops of rain.

Canvas of Contemplation

On a canvas blank, ideas collide,
With colors bright and joy that can't hide.
A splash of orange, a flick of blue,
Creating a scene that feels brand new.

Each brush stroke tells a tale so grand,
Of ninja squirrels in a marching band.
With giggles swirling 'round the hue,
It's a masterpiece emerging too!

A dab of mischief here and there,
Brushes dancing without a care.
A thoughtful giggle, a curious pout,
As words and colors swarm about.

And in the chaos, laughter sings,
Transforming thoughts to wondrous things.
On this canvas where dreams take flight,
Contemplation blossoms in pure delight.

Embracing the Unknown

In corners dark where giggles creep,
Adventures spark and secrets leap.
With shadows laughing, they tease the light,
As rascals dare to take a bite.

What's hiding there, beneath the bed?
A world of whim where thoughts are fed.
With sneaky rats in scarlet socks,
Whispers of mysteries in paradox.

The unknown winks, a playful tease,
While cackles rise like autumn leaves.
A treasure map sketched in bright crayon,
As they wander forth, unsure and drawn.

They twirl, they spin, through giggly gates,
In realms where witty fate awaits.
With hearts aglow in the wild and free,
Embracing unknowns, their destiny!

Pebbles of Intuition

Tiny stones roll in my brain,
Shaking out each silly strain.
Ideas bouncing to and fro,
Like rubber balls put on a show.

Cactus jokes and pickle puns,
Tickling me, oh what fun runs!
Thoughts that wobble, twist, and tease,
Like a clown on stilts with ease.

In the garden of my head,
Mushrooms dance, while coconuts spread.
Every whim that takes the stage,
Grows better with the laughter gauge.

As I build my castle high,
Out of jelly and blueberry pie.
My thoughts may scatter, trip, or trip,
But how they'd giggle on a trip!

Symphony of Mind

In my mind a tune so silly,
Playing notes that feel quite frilly.
Whistles, honks and gentle beats,
Tap dancing on my thought retreats.

A concerto of giggles, oh so grand,
With marshmallow violins and gumdrop bands.
The trombone slides with a blissful grin,
While the logic clarinet tries to fit in.

Each thought plays a prank, it seems,
Like juggling bubbles with funny dreams.
An orchestra of nonsense, a marvelous blend,
Even the cat joins in, ready to lend.

When the curtain drops, I roar with glee,
At the chaos that came to be.
The music fades, yet in my head,
The laughter lingers, lightly spread.

Lights in the Fog

In a fog so thick, thoughts peek out,
Like headlights in a weird doubt.
Shadows laugh and dance around,
Jokes scattered on the ground.

A jellyfish floats past my mind,
In the mist, it's quite unrefined.
Bumbling ideas, lost but bold,
Chasing each other, stories untold.

The truths are swirling, shimmery round,
Whispers of laughter seem to abound.
I trip over giggles, oh what a blast,
Each chuckle blurring the moments passed.

But then a light breaks through the grey,
Bringing with it a humorous sway.
Wisdom wrapped in a grin so wide,
Shows life's best jokes cannot be denied.

Pathways of Possibility

Twists and turns on my thought road,
With silly signs and a clownish code.
Each path leads to a giggle twist,
Where logic meets the jest-filled mist.

A fork in the road says, 'Pick your seat!'
One leads to cake, oh how sweet!
The other to a whimsical dance,
Where ideas prance in a playful trance.

Jumping puddles of random facts,
Wearing mismatched socks, imagine that!
Every step's a chance to play,
In the land of dreams and whimsy sway.

So grab a hat and take a stroll,
With laughter ringing, heart and soul.
Each direction a playful spree,
In possibilities wild and free!

Light and Shadow

In the garden where ideas sprout,
You'll find a gnome with a funny snout.
He tells jokes to the daisies around,
While the shadows giggle without making a sound.

A butterfly lands on his nose,
He sneezes loudly, then promptly doze.
The flowers laugh, they dance with glee,
As secrets drip like honey from a tree.

The sun shines bright, but the gnome stays cool,
Chasing thoughts in his whimsical pool.
He dives for wisdom, but comes up with a fish,
Who rants about life and its silly twists.

With a flip and a flap, the gnome throws it back,
"Wisdom is slippery, quite the trick track!"
The garden erupts in playful haze,
For laughter is sunlight, igniting bright days.

Tangles of Desire

In the maze of dreams, where wishes get stuck,
A cat in a hat finds a bit of luck.
He chases a thought like a wayward mouse,
But ends up munching on plans of the house.

A squirrel scurries, with nuts in tow,
He dreams of a treehouse, a tiny tableau.
With hands on his hips and a wink in his eye,
He declares, 'Why not? Let's give it a try!'

But building a dream takes some twist and shout,
While the cat yells, 'No! Put that nut down, Scout!'
And as the plans tangle like spaghetti strands,
They laugh at the chaos, forgetting their plans.

In this comedy of errors, joy reigns supreme,
For nothing is better than a shared silly dream.
With nuts and ideas all scattered about,
The laughter they share is what it's all about.

Unveiling the Veil

Behind the curtain, a chicken doth cluck,
With secrets to share, but it's just plain luck.
It struts with a giggle, proud as can be,
While the curtain ripples like waves in the sea.

A rabbit peeks in, with a curious glance,
"Are you hiding a secret or just showing off dance?"
The chicken looks puzzled, then fluffs out a feather,
"Perhaps it's a hat? Shall we wear them together?"

Oh, the laughter they share amongst the reveal,
As the rabbit dons feathers, what a quirky appeal!
In a world of veils, happiness blooms,
And wisdom tiptoes, disguised in costumes.

Yet the secrets unwrapped spill joy in a wave,
For the silliest notions make the best stories save.
Those antics we cherish, endless and grand,
In a play of fables, where giggles expand.

Wayward Winds of Wisdom

With a whoosh and a whirl, down the path they stroll,
A kite and a thought, sharing one common goal.
The wind whispers secrets, tickling the air,
While these two companions dance without a care.

"Catch me if you can!" the thought slyly quips,
As the kite swoops low, doing playful flips.
Through paper clouds, they dart and dip,
With laughter that echoes, not a moment to skip.

They soar over mountains and dodge the tall pines,
Finding treasures in laughter, not just in designs.
For the journey is wilder than a tumbleweed's spin,
And wisdom's not serious, it's woven with grin.

As twilight descends, they land with a plop,
With tales to tell, they'll never swap.
For every gust that fluffs and sways,
Is a reminder of joy in the playful ways.

Fledgling Notions

Tiny ideas sprout and grow,
With wiggles, jigs, and quite the show.
Like puppies chasing their own tails,
They leap about, leaving funny trails.

In jars with laughter, thoughts might stew,
Bubbling up with a giggling crew.
Each notion bounces like a ball,
Who knew they'd cause a silly brawl?

They wear tiny hats and dance on toes,
With mismatched shoes and silly bows.
The quirkiest bunch you've ever met,
Let's take a picture, don't forget!

So here we are, with thoughts galore,
Just watch them tumble, roll, and soar.
In worlds of whimsy, joy's the key,
Fledgling notions—wild and free!

Pollen of Possibility

Buzzing notions drift on air,
Chasing bees, without a care.
A sprinkle here, a giggle there,
What a sweet and fragrant flair!

Ideas flutter from flower to flower,
Turning seconds into an hour.
"A hat for a cat?" one thought quips,
While another dreams of giving fish trips.

With pollen grains from silly minds,
In hives of laughter, joy unwinds.
Dancing pollen, the silliest crew,
Crafting new visions—who knew they'd brew?

Let ideas buzz with no restraint,
In this meadow, we'll paint the quaint.
What's the rush? We'll let hearts sing,
With laughter's pollen, we'll grow anything!

The Fertile Ground of Imagination

Digging deep with a funny spade,
Planting jokes, making a parade.
Sprinkling giggles, plenty to share,
In this garden, there's humor in the air.

With carrots wearing tiny shoes,
And broccoli with colorful hues.
A vegetable dance, just watch them twirl,
Silly sights that make our minds whirl!

Beneath the soil, thoughts take hold,
Growing bright in shades of bold.
In the garden of fun, there's always room,
For wild ideas to brightly bloom.

So come and join this playful spree,
In fertile ground, where we're all free.
Let's dig for laughter, let ideas fly,
In our whimsical garden, oh my, oh my!

Sowing Seeds of Change

Tossing ideas like seeds in the breeze,
With each giggle, there's wild expertise.
"Let's change the world!" one notion shouts,
While another prances and jumps about.

Mixing colors, aiming for the stars,
Dreams take shape, like silly cars.
With wheels of laughter, and engines of fun,
Zooming and zipping—oh, what a run!

Whimsical plans sprout up from below,
Catching the sunlight, watch them glow.
"Who says we can't turn frowns to grins?"
With joy as our fuel, let the fun begin!

So let's sow together, side by side,
In the fields of mirth, we'll take a ride.
With every chuckle, let's rearrange,
The landscape of life, sowing seeds of change!

Flickers of Inspiration

In the attic of my mind, they play,
Tiny ideas like kids at a cafe.
One wears a hat, another a shoe,
They giggle and dance, so many to view.

A thought pops up like toast from a grill,
Sparks of brilliance, what a thrill!
One dreams of pizza, another of pie,
With toppings like dreams, they float by.

Jokes tumble out, in a whirlwind of cheer,
Laughter erupts, we hold it near.
Who knew a brain could be this much fun?
Like a party that's just begun!

So here's to the ideas, tiny and neat,
That hop on our minds, oh what a treat!
They light up the corners, never confined,
Flickers of joy in the ever-busy mind.

The Blooming Brain

In a garden of neurons, ideas sprout,
With petals of musings that twist about.
One shouts, "I'm a genius!" – what a claim,
While another whispers, "I'm just here for the fame."

Thoughts blossom bright, like daisies in June,
Some wear sunglasses, grooving to a tune.
While others just giggle at puns left to chance,
And twirl in delight like a silly dance.

"Let's grow some wild plans!" yells a cheeky one,
While others discuss how to bake cinnamon buns.
With nectar of laughter, they sip and they sip,
In this quirky domain, they eagerly trip.

So if your brain blooms — embrace it with glee,
Dancing with jesters, as silly as can be!
For each quirky notion is worth its own cheer,
In the garden of thoughts, let's all revere!

Harvesting New Horizons

In fields of the mind, where laughter grows,
New ideas sprout, like garden gnomes in rows.
We pluck them with glee, we toss them about,
Harvesting memories, what's that all about?

With a silly hat made from thoughts on a spree,
We shout, "Look at this one! It's dancing — whee!"
The more we collect, the funnier it seems,
As we weave them together to craft silly dreams.

New horizons appear, painted bright with our joy,
Where whimsies and wonders make silliness buoy.
So grab your cart, let's go on a quest,
To gather great giggles and jokes, the best!

With cartwheels of thoughts, we bound and we leap,
Each jest a treasure that we'll always keep.
Harvesting laughs, with laughter as gold,
In fields of imagination, let's be bold!

Tiny Thoughts Take Flight

Tiny thoughts take off on the breeze,
Like little balloons that dance with such ease.
One's a funny face, another's a frog,
They soar through the air, oh what a smog!

With wings made of giggles, they flutter and play,
Chasing each other in a whimsical way.
"Catch me if you can!" one shouts with a grin,
As they tumble through clouds filled with friendly din.

"Let's land on a pancake!" cries a bright spark,
"Or hop on a cupcake, let's leave a mark!"
The world is their playground, so silly, so free,
Tiny thoughts buzzing — just look and you'll see!

So give them some room, let them soar and go wild,
For in each little thought lies a giggling child.
As they flit and they fly, we laugh and delight,
Embracing the joy of each whimsical flight.

Moonlit Reflections

In the glow of the night, I ponder,
Do frogs in the pond ever just wander?
Do they have deep talks about the day,
Or croak silly songs in their own froggy way?

A cat on the fence, looking so wise,
Pretending to see through the darkening skies.
With a flick of its tail and a stretch of its paw,
Is it plotting a scheme? Oh, I bet that it's raw!

With stars overhead making a fuss,
I wonder if they ever ride on a bus.
Do they gossip and giggle, dance up so high,
Or just blink their bright lights and wave us goodbye?

The moon grins down on this curious scene,
While shadows debate if they've been here or seen.
Is the night just a joke that the world plays round?
With laughter and wonder, magic is found.

Cracks in the Soil

In the garden where weeds dance in cheer,
A worm reads the news, or so I hear.
It's gossip from roots about clouds up above,
Or tales of a snail and its slow-moving love.

Dandelions wishing they'd change their attire,
They puff out their seeds, like confetti on fire.
Do they giggle as breezes sweep them away,
Dreaming of places where they'd rather play?

The ants have a meeting all lined up in rows,
Discussing their plans, as each one just knows.
With crumbs at their feet and a map in their mind,
They're plotting a feast, for a party designed!

Through cracks in the soil, mysteries prance,
Little critters all join in the fun-loving dance.
With laughter and soil, they swirl and they twirl,
In this tiny domain, the chaos unfurl.

Cascades of Awareness

In the stream of thought, a fish jumps about,
With scales made of laughter, and giggles, no doubt.
It circles around, with a twinkle and flick,
Planning a wet joke or a slippery trick.

A frog on a lily pad ponders what's next,
Whether to leap or to just be perplexed.
Does it croak out a pun to the dragonfly crew,
Or offer up sage advice on what not to do?

Bubbles of wisdom float up to the sky,
Is it just me, or are fish prone to lie?
Do they whisper of treasure beneath them each day,
While plotting their moves in a rascally way?

Cascades of thought in a giggling stream,
Where awareness meets whimsy, a fanciful dream.
Here laughter is plenty, and ideas take wing,
In a world made of wonder, where joy's the king!

Harvest of Dreams

In the fields of my mind, where daydreams are sown,
I gather the laughter, from seeds I've outgrown.
With a tote bag of giggles, I pluck thoughts with flair,
And toss them like confetti, high up in the air.

The scarecrow hums a tune, slightly off-key,
While worms groove along in their underground spree.
Do they know they're the stars of a soil-based show?
Dancing to rhythms of the roots down below?

Pumpkins are plotting a playful surprise,
With winks and sly smiles, they light up their eyes.
Are they plotting to roll down the hill for a thrill,
Or merely a gag that's part of their drill?

In this harvest, we gather joy, not a frown,
Crafting a feast from the glee we've found.
For laughter is plenty, and dreams are aglow,
Let's celebrate whims as we reap and we sow!

Tender Insights

In the garden, a thought did sprout,
It asked, 'What's this fuss all about?'
With a giggle, it wiggled, and danced,
Making all the flowers quite entranced.

The bumblebee buzzed with a grin,
Said, 'You know, you've quite the spin!'
But the daisy just rolled her eyes wide,
'You think you're clever, but we all hide!'

Yet the thought kept bouncing all around,
With every laugh, new friends it found.
'Let's throw a party, what could go wrong?'
As the wind sang their silly song.

So gather 'round, let's make it clear,
A giggle grows if we all cheer!
Among the blooms, let joy unfold,
With jokes and puns worth their weight in gold.

Flourishing Notions

In a pot, a wild whim took flight,
Claiming itself a bird of delight!
With roots in the dirt and dreams in the air,
It chirped, 'Can I sing? Can I dare?'

The tomato laughed, 'You're not quite a bird,
But you do say the silliest word!'
And the mint chimed in with a twist of lime,
'Oh, darling thought, you're simply sublime!'

So they formed a band, strumming on leaves,
Tickling each other, sharing their thieves.
But the basil rolled over, all sleepy and slow,
'Can't you keep it down? I've got to grow!'

Undeterred, they danced on, full of cheer,
Knowing that laughter is the sweetest ear.
On this stage of earth, let humor take flight,
For growing ideas feels absolutely right.

Branches of Memory

A squirrel once forgot where it hid,
A thought of an acorn, a well-kept grid.
It climbed up high, then lost all shame,
'This tree looks different, what's her name?'

The oak shook her leaves, in a fit of giggles,
'You lost your lunch, or perhaps some wiggles?'
The nutty notion rolled in the dew,
'Perhaps I'll plan a feasting crew!'

So they gathered, the critters and friends,
To share the jokes as their laughter transcends.
Yet all they found were a few old nuts,
And a worm who replied, 'Oh, such big guts!'

So memories grow, like wild vines in spring,
To remind us of laughter, that sweet little thing.
Every twist and turn, a story to swap,
Together we're blooming, ready to pop!

Awakening Whispers

In the early dusk, a whisper was heard,
'Twas a tickle, a nudge, like a chatty bird!
It said, 'Wake up, there's fun to be had,
Let's tumble and roll; it's sure to be rad!'

A sleepy little sprout, stifled a yawn,
'But what about the sunlight, and the dawn?'
Yet the voice giggled, 'Just stretch a bit,
You see, the world's rosy, let's not sit!'

They frolicked beneath a zany night sky,
With the stars twinkling, oh so spry!
'What if we leap? What if we play?'
As the moonbox chuckled, casting beams in the fray.

And so they danced, in a world full of dreams,
Filled with laughs and flamboyant themes.
Those whispers of joy are what keep us near,
For life is a riddle, be silly, my dear!

Flourish and Fade

In the garden of ideas, I planted a joke,
It sprouted a laugh, then it choked on smoke.
With a punchline like lettuce, it started to bloom,
But the humor turned sour, like expired perfume.

I watered my puns with a bucket of jest,
Each chuckle I earned, I thought I was blessed.
But weeds of confusion crept in with the night,
Now my garden's just wild, oh where is the light?

Sunshine of laughter, it flickers and fades,
As I trip on my thoughts, my sanity wades.
With roots of mischief growing deep in my brain,
I laugh at the chaos, but is it in vain?

The flowers of folly just dance in the breeze,
With petals of giggles, they tickle the trees.
In this patch of the wacky, I swirl and I spin,
Gardening madness, oh let the fun begin!

Whispers in the Wind

A thought blew by, cheeky and spry,
It tickled my ear, made me wonder why.
I chased it around, like a dog with a ball,
But it giggled away, oh where is my call?

The breeze tells secrets, whispers so sly,
Of dreams left unharvested, oh me, oh my!
I raised up my hands to catch every sigh,
But thoughts are like feathers, they drift and they fly.

In the meadow of musings, I twirled and I spun,
But the wind just chuckled, "You're not the only one!"
A flock of old notions joined in the chase,
Each one was a riddle, wearing a face.

With visions so fickle, they waltzed through the morn,
Dancing with giggles, the ideas were born.
So I'll sway in this current, with humor so light,
Let thoughts come a-whispering, day into night.

Enchanted Seeds

I planted some dreams in a pot of pure fun,
With wishes for laughter, and jokes on the run.
But sprouting from soil came a pickle and pie,
Now I'm stuck in a kitchen, oh me, oh my!

The muffins tell stories; the biscuits just grin,
While the oatmeal winks like it's wearing a chin.
In this magical plot, the flavors collide,
With salsa that dances and fries that slide.

The veggies are chatting in a comical way,
Making plans for a roast that'll brighten the day.
I chuckle at cabbage, its leaves in a twist,
And lettuce just whispers, "Let's make a list!"

In this enchanted garden where laughter can sprout,
Every meal's a magic show, without a doubt.
So gather your spoons, let the giggles ensue,
For cooking's a plot where the funny runs true!

Tides of Thought

In the ocean of wonder where ideas collide,
The waves carry whispers of nonsense and pride.
I surf on the ripples of laughter divine,
Riding high on a joke, like a fish on a vine.

With tides that come rolling, I'm swept in the flow,
A mermaid of humor, where giggles can grow.
But beware of the shoals where the seriousness linger,
For there lies a crab with a terrible stinger.

I build castles of puns on the beach of my brain,
With moats full of chuckles, my laughter's my gain.
The tide pulls me back, but I wave it goodbye,
As I dance with the dolphins, just me and the sky.

So come join the frolic, let's swim in the sea,
Where thoughts tide and whirl, wild and free.
Together we'll ride waves of whimsy and cheer,
As we craft every giggle to last through the year!

Tendrils of Emotion

In the garden of my head, it's quite a scene,
Thoughts sprout up like weeds, if you know what I mean.

One worries of the weather, another fears the frost,
Chasing all the bunnies, see what's gained and lost.

A sprinkle of green onions, and a radish on the side,
Who knew that such small roots could hold a world inside?
They sway and dance in breezes, with gossip on their tongues,
Debating life and choices, oh what fun it surely flungs!

There's a flower that's a joker, with petals made of jokes,

Telling witty puns to all the curious folks.
"What's the drama in the soil? It's just a little mud!"
And all the other plants roll their eyes with joy and thud.

Yet amidst the laughter blooms, there sprouts a lot of fear,

What if the gardener came, wielding scissors near?
But with a chuckle, they decide to take a chance,
For every snip could lead to quite a fun new dance!

Pathways of Perception

In the maze of what I think, there's a squirrel in a hat,
Doing flips and tricks while my mind goes splat!
Each thought a little acorn, much too heavy to crack,
But look, a cheeky chipmunk steals my focus back!

Rabbits hop down avenues of bright, silly ideas,
Wearing shoes that squeak, oh how they bring the cheers!

One wears socks that slip, another has a crown,
Together they form parades beneath the sky so brown.

Tickling bouncy brain waves, like waves that crash the shore,
Thoughts rise and fall like tides, always wanting more.
But then a cloud of confusion floats entirely on by,
And suddenly that squirrel has way too much pie!

In the pathways of my mind, there's laughter everywhere,

With riddles, jesters, stunts, and lots of whimsical flair.
So if you find it tangled, just embrace each twist and shout,
For every slip and tumble leads to fun — there's not a doubt!

Luminous Beacons

What's shining in the dark? A lantern with a grin,
It lights up silly songs, and causes laughter to begin.
With jokes and dashes of glitter, it dances in the night,
Tickling all the shadows with its burst of sheer delight.

Each glowing thought a candle, flickering but bold,
Sharing secrets of the world that never gets too old.
A firefly named Bob blinks a message from afar,
"Life's a bright adventure, come ride with me, ha-ha!"

In the midst of all this giggling, watch out for the bees,
They buzz around with puns, as if it's all a breeze.
One amidst the flowers claims it's honey ruled by fun,
While others drop sweet nectar; oh, where have they all run?

To chase the light of laughter, just follow the glow,
For even in the darkest times, it teaches you to flow.
Paths of joy will lead you down, where humor, friendship bind,
And every glowing beacon is a thought that's free and kind!

Unraveled Threads of Thought

There's yarn spread out like rumors, in a basket full of dreams,
Each thread a silly notion, or so it often seems.
The cat rolls in the colors, knitting chaos with a purr,
Twisting up those bright ideas, oh, what a fuzzy blur!

A spool of tangled laughter, spiraled up in knots,
Brings forth the merry mishaps — forget-me-not thoughts!
Each pull of a loose strand unravels more to find,
A tapestry of giggles, a fabric interlined.

Beware the wobbly notions, those that try to dance,
They trip over their own tails, oh, still, they take a chance!

Patched together stories, from little snippets torn,
Are laughed about in circles, oh shouldn't have been worn!

So raise a toast to all of this, a colorful parade,
For every silly fiber makes the best of our charade.
Unraveling those threads of thought can lead to endless fun,
In this knitted tapestry, there's joy for everyone!

Burgeoning Dreams

In the garden of my mind, ideas sprout,
Some are wild, others shy, full of doubt.
A silly notion wore a grass-green coat,
While a quirky one tried to learn to float.

Potatoes dream of flying in the sky,
While peas in their pods laugh and sigh.
The carrots debate why they're underground,
And the lettuce just waves, all around.

Bananas polish thoughts, shiny and bright,
While brussels sprouts gossip late into the night.
Seeds of giggles burst, create new sounds,
As they dance in the soil, joy abounds.

With every wacky thought that blooms and grows,
I find laughter where the silliness flows.
The more I water dreams, the funnier they seem,
Cultivating hilarity, my own funny dream.

Crossroads of Creativity

At the junction where ideas collide,
A pineapple skateboard speaks with pride.
A cactus in shades claims it's so cool,
While a turnip asks, 'Is this some kind of school?'

With crayons sprinting in the open air,
And paper planes folding in a daring flare.
A cupcake with sprinkles, yelling, 'Let's go!'
Dreams zip by, putting on a show.

A silly goose leads a parade of fun,
While a daffodil says, 'I'm number one!'
With tangents and twists that spin round and round,
In this odd circus of thoughts, laughter is found.

So here I stand at this crossroad of plays,
Where quirky ideas bounce in a maze.
I take a step forward, arms wide and free,
Embracing the nonsense that's calling to me.

Still Waters of Insight

In the pond of my thoughts, ripples arise,
A frog with a monocle offers advice.
'Jump in, take a splash, take the plunge now!'
While a fish in a bowtie says, 'You'll learn how!'

The catfish read physics, it's quite absurd,
While a turtle writes novels, that's the word.
They ponder the meaning of life underwater,
And hold deep debates over a fishy fritter.

The lily pads giggle at the wise old owl,
Who offers up riddles, with a serious scowl.
'Think outside the pond, that's the trick, you see?'
Calls the bowl of goldfish, with profound glee.

Yet, still I float in this thinking pool,
Embracing the nonsense, that's my own rule.
In waters of wit, so calm and so fine,
The laughter bubbles up like a good vintage wine.

Gardens of Reflection

In a garden of mirth, thoughts grow quite strange,
Where mushrooms wear hats, and fairness is a range.
The blooms whisper secrets beneath the bright sun,
While worms debate which flower is more fun.

With daisies doing flips, and roses that sway,
The garden of jest leads us all astray.
A sunflower jokes, 'I'm the tallest here!'
While the violets giggle, filled with good cheer.

Bumblebees buzz about with delight,
As the spinach sings songs late into the night.
A dancing toad serenades a fat bee,
In this playful patch where we're all wild and free.

As I wander this maze of laughter's sweet glow,
I find joy in blooms, where the quirkiest grow.
In gardens of laughter, thoughts twist and twine,
Reflecting the silly, a garden divine.

The Unfurled Scroll of Innovation

A quirky idea wakes up at dawn,
With a coffee cup, it stretches and yawns.
It dances on paper, it skips on the ink,
Dreams of inventions that make people think.

A toaster that toasts while reading the news,
Or socks that just sing when you wear your shoes.
Each thought's a little jester, making us grin,
Innovation's the circus, and we're all invited in.

From flying burritos to chairs that hug tight,
Every wild concept brings laughter and light.
So grab your quill, let's create quite a show,
For comedy blooms where ingenuity flows.

In the garden of wits, let's plant wild seeds,
Watch humor sprout just like unkempt weeds.
Let's dig up the laughter, let joy fill the air,
With funny inventions, we've got wit to spare.

Garden of Perception

In a patch of ideas where laughter is sown,
The flowers of nonsense have brightly grown.
With tulips in tutus and daisies in hats,
We can't help but giggle at these curious chats.

The sun shines an orange, the clouds puff up pink,
As dandelions whisper, 'Let's all have a drink!'
The veggies are gossiping, lettuce and peas,
While carrots debate who has the best knees.

Here's where the rhubarb tells jokes to the thyme,
And everyone giggles; it's truly sublime.
So step in the garden, let your mind stray,
Where laughter grows louder with each passing day.

With weeds full of wisdom and blooms filled with cheer,
Our minds can take flight, there's nothing to fear.
Let's harvest this joy, let it all unfold,
In the garden of jesters, laughter is gold.

Tending to Mental Gardens

Pull weeds of worry, plant seeds of delight,
Water your visions, let laughter ignite.
Grab your trowel of humor, let's dig in the dirt,
Where thoughts grow like daisies, and no one gets hurt.

We'll prune back the doubts, they've grown way too tall,
And let in the giggles that bounce off the wall.
With garden gnomes chuckling, we'll sow joy by the patch,
Finding wisdom in mishaps — oh, what a great catch!

The sun will burst forth with warmth and with cheer,
As we dance with the ideas that flourish right here.
A sprinkle of nonsense, a dash of good fun,
In mental gardens, laughter has won!

Let's harvest our thoughts, with humor as our tool,
Where silliness reigns and the wise are the fools.
So come, take a stroll, let your mind wander free,
In these gardens of giggles, there's plenty for me!

Dreams in the Soil

Beneath the ground where silliness thrives,
Lie dreams that sprout and take crazy dives.
With roots of ambition that tickle the toes,
Each thought is a plunge into laughter's repose.

The earth whispers secrets to those who will hear,
"Plant your wild notions, let go of your fear!"
But one tiny sprout had a mind of its own,
Chose to become a wacky garden gnome!

Next to daisies discussing the latest fashion,
And tulips with glasses, all filled with compassion.
The laughter erupts like a fountain in spring,
As dreams take their flight, and the joy's on the wing.

So let's dig in this soil of giggles and glee,
Where dreams bloom in color, as bright as can be.
In this garden of funny, let's never grow old,
For the dreams that we nurture will always be bold.

Roots of Reflection

In the garden of ideas, I dig a hole,
A shovelful of nonsense, it takes a toll.
My thoughts grow like weeds, wild and free,
Oh, where's my lunch? Is it lost in this tree?

I plant a few giggles, let them take root,
Adding in a punchline, who would dispute?
Nature's so quirky, it cracks me up,
Branches of laughter, overflowing cup.

I water with mustard, sprinkle some cheese,
Hope my reflections will flow with the breeze.
Roots intertwining, they tangle and dance,
Even my worries seem to take a chance.

With each silly notion that starts to sprout,
I'm busy laughing instead of a pout.
In this quirky garden, I'll happily thrive,
Growing my laughter, oh, how I strive!

Blossoming Ideas

In the spring of my whims, the blooms start to grow,
Each petal a thought, colors all in a row.
My mind's like a flower shop, chaos for sale,
Every bright hue tells a different tale.

I prune back the frowns, make room for delight,
Nonsense will sprout with the morning light.
A daisy says, "Why so serious, friend?"
Petals of laughter, let's never end!

The bees buzz along, they're friends of my muse,
Stealing my thoughts, what a sneaky ruse!
But the buzzing makes me giggle, it's true,
As I plant silly scenes in the morning dew.

So let's tend to this patch of imagination,
With laughter and puns, it's my dedication.
As colors collide in a whimsical play,
Blossoming bright, chase the worries away!

Quiet Contemplations

In moments of stillness, I ponder the view,
Shadows and whispers, what's out there to do?
A thought wanders by, in a fluffy white hat,
Is it a plan? Or just a curious cat?

I sit in a quiet nook, lost in my mind,
Musing on quandaries of every kind.
Do fish laugh at jokes? Or just swim along?
Let them tell the tales, they've got it all wrong!

The clouds pass overhead, they giggle and cheer,
Whispers of nonsense, joy that I hear.
I scratch my head softly, as rain starts to fall,
What if umbrellas could dance? Would they twirl at all?

In this laughter-laden space, I take a pause,
Thoughts romp around, and give me applause.
With each silly notion, my smile expands,
Quiet contemplations, oh how life demands!

Germination of Mind

In the quirky realm of the brain's little plot,
A seed of a joke is growing on the spot.
With laughter as fertilizer, I'll have to confess,
The punchlines are sprouting, it's anyone's guess!

In this funny farm, I hoe with delight,
Ideas turn ridiculous, banish the fright.
What if spaghetti could dance at a ball?
I'd be the first to invite them, after all!

Worms in the dirt are my buddies today,
They wiggle and giggle in their grand ballet.
Thoughts seep through the soil, biking in line,
I mix up my puns, like grape and brine.

So let's cultivate laughter in sunlight and rain,
As the garden of humor drives away the mundane.
With each ticklish concept that comes into sight,
Germination is thriving, oh what a delight!

Cultivating Creative Sparks

In a garden of ideas, I plant my dreams,
With water from laughter and sunlight from schemes.
The weeds of doubt, I swiftly pull out,
As giggles take root, and my worries scream shout.

A flower of nonsense starts to bloom bright,
Dancing with joy in the warm morning light.
Bees buzzing puns, tickling the air,
Who knew that ideas could grow on a dare?

The soil is rich with a fertilizer laugh,
Fertile for musings, both silly and daft.
Each thought a petal, spinning with cheer,
Watch out world, there's a new voice near!

So come wave your wand, sprinkle some glee,
And join me in planting this whimsical spree.
For each little giggle can sprout to delight,
In our kooky garden, all ideas take flight.

The Invisible Forest Within

Deep in my mind, a forest has grown,
With branches of whimsy, and laughter is sown.
The trunks are all thoughts, quirky and vast,
Whispers of nonsense flit by like a blast.

Squirrels of humor scamper up high,
Chasing the dreams that float by with a sigh.
Each leaf is a joke, fluttering free,
Tickling the breeze with absurdity.

The roots intertwine, tickling my brain,
While the mushrooms pop up, causing sweet pain.
In this wild grove, all troubles are blurred,
Who knew being silly could be so absurd?

So venture inside to this jungle so fine,
Where giggles and fancies align in a line.
A canopy brightens the thoughts that are there,
In this invisible forest, you'll find joy to share.

Petals of Potential

Oh, tiny buds, with the dreams that they bare,
Each color a thought, floating light as air.
Petals unfurling, with giggles they burst,
Tickling convention, quenching the thirst.

With rain of ideas showering down,
Blooming up moments, they'll wear a crown.
A daisy of laughter, a rose made of fun,
Growing wild in the light of the sun.

Bees dance around with a buzz and a grin,
Pollinating giggles, let the chaos begin!
The garden of whimsy, all tends to delight,
See how they flourish, oh what a sight!

So grab a bouquet of the strange and the weird,
Here's to the bloom of thoughts that appeared.
Plucking the petals, for each silly wink,
In the delightful dance of "What do you think?"

A Tapestry of Emerging Concept

In the loom of my mind, ideas entwine,
Threads of the silly, weaves so divine.
Fraying the edges, as laughter sets in,
Creating a quilt, where the giggles begin.

Stitching together, the charm and the cheer,
A patchwork of nonsense, oh so sincere.
Quirky and whimsical, patterns collide,
In this colorful madness, there's nowhere to hide.

Fabrics of laughter, now cover my walls,
Rugged with joy, as the humor enthralls.
Each woven distraction, a journey anew,
In the tapestry bright, I'm tangled with you.

So let's toss those threads, let them weave and twirl,
In the fabric of fantasy, let joy unfurl.
We'll quilt all our whims into one happy dance,
Creating a masterpiece, let's take a chance!

www.ingramcontent.com/pod-product-compliance
Lightning Source LLC
Chambersburg PA
CBHW072149200426
43209CB00051B/930